MARY BERRY'S
FAMILY RECIPES

Macdonald

Editorial manager
Chester Fisher
Series editor
Jim Miles
Editor
Linda Sonntag
Designer
Robert Wheeler
Production
Penny Kitchenham

© Macdonald Educational Ltd 1979

Text © Thames Television Ltd 1979

Published in association with
Thames Television's programme
After Noon Plus edited by Catherine
Freeman

First published 1979
Macdonald Educational Ltd
Holywell House
Worship Street
London EC2A 2EN

ISBN 356 06204 X (paperback edition)
ISBN 356 06284 8 (cased edition)

Contents

5 Introduction
6 Soup and good beginnings
12 Chicken
16 Family meat dishes
24 Vegetables
29 Hot puddings
34 Cold puddings
43 Ice cream
47 Cakes and baking
57 Tasty tit-bits
63 Index

Introduction

Welcome to *After Noon Plus* and to the latest cook book of family recipes. As you will have noticed, the programmes now follow a different pattern; I no longer have the help and encouragement I used to have from Judith Chalmers (how I miss her!). But I do now occasionally have the chance to invite a viewer with a cooking problem along to the studios so that we can make whatever dish is creating difficulties for her.

Some of these recipes and many more from past and future programmes are included in this book and I always add my 'cook's tip' – which is a piece of useful advice or some short-cut I've discovered while cooking the dish for my own family.

As usual I've tried to make the recipes as simple as possible and given you the ingredients in both metric and imperial measurements. In addition to the colour photographs, expertly shot by John Lee, I've also included a selection of line drawings to clarify the method.

My thanks as always go to Clare Blunt who helps me to prepare the programmes and try out all the recipes and to my family whose enthusiastic reception of my cooking makes it all the more rewarding.

Soup and good beginnings

Fresh leek soup

2 oz butter	*50 gm butter*
1½ lb leeks, cleaned and finely chopped	*675 gm leeks, cleaned and finely chopped*
1 oz flour	*25 gm flour*
1 pint home-made stock or 2 chicken stock cubes dissolved in 1 pint water	*600 ml home-made stock or 2 chicken stock cubes dissolved in 600 ml water*
salt and pepper	*salt and pepper*
½ pint milk	*300 ml milk*
a little single cream if liked	*a little single cream if liked*

Add single cream before serving for special occasions, about ¼ pint (150 ml) is plenty.

Melt the butter in a large saucepan. Add the leeks and fry gently stirring occasionally without browning for 5 minutes. Stir in the flour and cook for 2 minutes.

Gradually add the stock, stirring continually. Add seasoning and milk, bring to the boil and simmer for 40 minutes. Taste and check seasoning and if liked add a little cream. Serves 4.

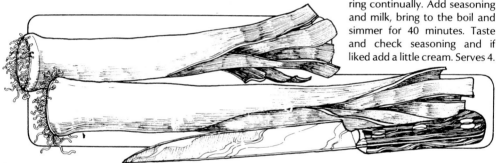

Good carrot soup

1 lb carrots	*450 gm carrots*
1 small onion	*1 small onion*
1 oz butter	*25 gm butter*
1¼ pints chicken stock or 1¼ pints water and 2 chicken stock cubes	*750 ml chicken stock or 750 ml water and 2 chicken stock cubes*
3 strips of orange peel	*3 strips of orange peel*
1 bayleaf	*1 bayleaf*
salt and pepper	*salt and pepper*

For special occasions add swirls of cream or yoghurt to the soup before serving.

Peel and slice the carrots and onions. Melt the butter in a pan and add the vegetables, cover and cook gently for 5 to 10 minutes. Pour on the stock or water and stock cubes and add the strips of orange peel (take the peel from the orange with a potato peeler). Add bayleaf and seasoning and bring to the boil. Cover and simmer for about 15 minutes or until the carrots are tender.

Remove the bayleaf then sieve or liquidize the soup in a blender. Taste and check seasoning and if the soup should be too thick, thin down with a little extra stock. Serves 4.

Frugal soup

8 oz sprouts and trimmings
1 leek
1 oz butter
¾ pint water
1 chicken stock cube
1 oz flour
½ pint milk
large pinch grated nutmeg
salt and pepper

225 gm sprouts and
  trimmings
1 leek
25 gm butter
450 ml water
1 chicken stock cube
25 gm flour
300 ml milk
large pinch grated nutmeg
salt and pepper

Cut down on waste by using the out-side leaves of sprouts for this soup. They do not detract from its beauti-ful flavour.

Wash and roughly chop the sprouts and trimmings, thoroughly wash the leek and cut in slices.

Melt the butter in a pan and add the leek, cover and cook gently for 5 minutes, add the water, stock cube and sprouts and bring to the boil. Simmer uncovered for 15 minutes or until tender, then sieve or puree in the blender.

Blend the flour with a little of the milk, then stir in the remainder. Return the soup to the pan and stir in the milk and flour. Bring to the boil, stirring until thickened, season with nutmeg and salt and pepper. If the soup should be a little too thick thin down with stock or milk. Serves 4.

Cheese soufflé

1½ oz butter
1¼ oz flour
½ pint hot milk
salt and pepper
1 level teaspoon made
    mustard
4 oz strong Cheddar cheese,
    grated
4 large eggs

40 gm butter
40 gm flour
300 ml hot milk
salt and pepper
1 level teaspoon made
    mustard
100 gm strong Cheddar
    cheese, grated
4 large eggs

Heat the oven to 375°F, 190°C, Gas No. 5 and place a baking sheet in it. Melt the butter in a pan, stir in the flour and cook for 2 minutes without browning. Remove the pan from the heat and stir in the hot milk. Return to the heat and bring to the boil, stirring until thickened, then add the seasoning and mustard and leave to cool.

Stir in the cheese. If preferred use 3 oz (75 gm) strong Cheddar cheese and 1 oz (25 gm) grated Parmesan. Separate the eggs and beat the yolks one at a time into the cheese sauce. Whisk the egg whites with a rotary hand or electric whisk until stiff, but not dry. Stir one heaped tablespoonful into the cheese sauce and then carefully fold in the remainder.

Pour into a buttered 2 pint (a good litre) soufflé dish, run a teaspoon around the edge of the dish and bake on a hot baking sheet in the centre of the oven for about 40 minutes until well risen and golden brown. Serve at once. Serves 3 to 4.

Variations

Choose any flavouring and add to the mixture before the egg yolks.
Ham: add 4 to 6 oz (100 to 175 gm) ham or boiled bacon, finely chopped.
Fish: add 4 to 6 oz (100 to 175 gm) finely flaked cooked smoked haddock.
Shellfish: add 4 oz (100 gm) peeled prawns or shrimps.
Mushroom: add 8 oz (225 gm) finely chopped mushrooms, cooked in 1 oz (25 gm) butter.
Spinach: add 1 lb (450 gm) cooked finely chopped spinach with a pinch of nutmeg and topped with a little grated cheese.

This makes a delicious light lunch, but if you prefer, serve it as a first course baked in small ramekins. In smaller dishes the soufflé will only take about 20 minutes to cook.

Cheese aigrettes

1 oz butter
¼ pint water
2 oz self-raising flour
1 egg yolk
1 egg
2 oz mature Cheddar cheese, grated
salt
cayenne pepper

25 gm butter
150 ml water
50 gm self-raising flour
1 egg yolk
1 egg
50 gm mature Cheddar cheese, grated
salt
cayenne pepper

Serve as a savoury course or as a snack with drinks.

Put butter and water in a small saucepan and bring to the boil. Remove from the heat and add the flour, beat well until the mixture is glossy and leaves the sides of the pan clean, cool slightly.

Lightly mix the yolk and the egg together and beat into the mixture a little at a time. Stir in the cheese, salt and a pinch of cayenne pepper, check seasoning.

When required, drop the mixture in heaped teaspoonfuls into hot deep fat and fry gently until golden brown, turning once. Lift out and drain on kitchen paper. Serve at once. To freeze: open-freeze then pack in a container, label and return to freezer. To serve, defrost for about 2 hours at room temperature and then heat in a hot oven at 425°F, 220°C, Gas No. 7 for about 10 minutes. Makes about 16 cheese aigrettes.

Melon and prawns in sour cream

1 small melon
a little shredded lettuce
4 oz frozen prawns, thawed
5 oz carton soured cream,
   chilled
1 rounded teaspoon
   chopped mint
small sprigs of mint

1 small melon
a little shredded lettuce
100 gm frozen prawns, thawed
150 ml carton soured cream,
   chilled
1 rounded teaspoon
   chopped mint
small sprigs of mint

Cut the melon in half and remove all the seeds. Scoop out the flesh into balls and leave to chill in the refrigerator.

Place a little shredded lettuce in the bottom of 6 glasses.

Thoroughly dry the prawns on kitchen paper and drain off any juice from the melon. Put in a bowl with the cream and chopped mint and blend lightly. Divide between the glasses, garnish each with a small sprig of mint and serve at once. Serves 6.

I often do this easy first course when melons are reasonably priced. Serve a non-fruity dessert to follow. Take care to thaw the prawns slowly in the fridge and dab off every drop of liquid before blending with the cream.

Chicken

Paprika chicken

4 chicken breasts
2 tablespoons salad oil
1 oz butter
1 onion, chopped
2 level tablespoons paprika
  pepper
1 oz flour
¼ pint stock
¼ pint dry cider
5 tablespoons sherry
1 level teaspoon tomato
  puree
salt and pepper
6 oz small button
  mushrooms
¼ pint soured cream
chopped parsley
fried sliced mushrooms

4 chicken breasts
2 tablespoons salad oil
25 gm butter
1 onion, chopped
2 level tablespoons paprika
  pepper
25 gm flour
150 ml stock
150 ml dry cider
5 tablespoons sherry
1 level teaspoon tomato
  puree
salt and pepper
175 gm small button
  mushrooms
150 ml soured cream
chopped parsley
fried sliced mushrooms

A rich creamy chicken dish delicious served with rice, noodles or new potatoes and a green salad or broccoli.

Remove the skin from the chicken breasts. Heat the oil in a large shallow pan, add the butter and then fry the chicken quickly to slightly brown. Remove from the pan and drain on kitchen paper. Add the onion and paprika to the pan and fry for 2 minutes. Blend in the flour and cook for a further minute. Remove from the heat and stir in the stock, cider and sherry. Return to the heat and simmer until thick. Add the tomato puree and seasoning to the sauce, stir well and then return the chicken breasts to the pan; cover and simmer gently for 30 minutes, turning once.

Wash the mushrooms, add to the pan and simmer for a further 5 minutes.

When ready to serve, lift the chicken breasts onto a serving dish and stir the soured cream into the sauce, then pour over the chicken. Sprinkle with parsley and garnish the dish with fried sliced mushrooms. Serves 4.

Chicken galantine

3½ lb chicken	1.5 kg chicken
12 oz lean pork, minced	350 gm lean pork
12 oz pork sausagemeat	350 gm pork sausagemeat
1 small onion, minced	1 small onion, minced
2 cloves garlic, crushed	2 cloves garlic, crushed
1½ oz fresh breadcrumbs	40 gm fresh breadcrumbs
1 egg	1 egg
large pinch dried thyme	large pinch dried thyme
1 teaspoon salt	1 teaspoon salt
plenty of ground black pepper	plenty of ground black pepper
4 oz slice cooked ham	100 gm slice cooked ham
1 oz green stuffed olives	25 gm green stuffed olives

Although this takes time to do it is worth it for a party. If you give your butcher lots of warning he may well bone the chicken for you.

Bone the chicken. Make a cut along the length of the backbone and with a small sharp knife cut the flesh away from the bones down each side. When you come to the wing knuckle cut it away from the carcass. Scrape the meat off the bone down to the first joint. Cut off there and then repeat with the other side.

With the leg joint, cut away again at the carcass, but scrape the meat away from the two bones of the leg, turning the flesh inside out as you go. Carefully cut the meat away from the rest of the carcass until you can lift it out. Remove any excess lumps of fat and lay the chicken skin-side down on a board, turning the legs back into shape. Use the carcass for making stock or soup.

Heat the oven to 375°F, 190°C, Gas No. 5.

Mix together the pork, sausage meat, onion, garlic, breadcrumbs, egg, thyme and salt and pepper. Spread half this mixture down the centre of the chicken.

Cut the ham into ¾ inch (2 cm) strips lengthwise and lay on top of the stuffing interspersed with the olives. Cover with the remaining pork mixture and wrap the chicken over. Turn over and shape to resemble a chicken, place in a meat roasting tin and very lightly spread the breast with a little butter.

Bake in the centre of the oven for 1½ hours, basting occasionally.

Lift out and place on a dish to cool. When quite cold put in the refrigerator until required. Then serve sliced with various salads. Serves 10.

13

Roast chicken with apricot and nut stuffing

2 oz dried apricots
1 oz butter
1 onion, chopped
2 oz brown breadcrumbs
1 oz peanuts or cashew nuts,
    coarsely chopped
grated rind of $\frac{1}{2}$ a lemon
1 level teaspoon brown sugar
1 rounded tablespoon
    chopped parsley
salt and pepper
$3\frac{1}{2}$ lb chicken

50 gm dried apricots
25 gm butter
1 onion, chopped
50 gm brown breadcrumbs
25 gm peanuts or cashew
    nuts, coarsely chopped
grated rind of $\frac{1}{2}$ a lemon
1 level teaspoon brown sugar
1 rounded tablespoon
    chopped parsley
salt and pepper
1·5 kg chicken

Place the apricots in a small bowl, cover with water and leave to soak overnight. Drain and place in a saucepan with water just to cover and simmer gently for about 20 minutes until just cooked. Drain well, reserving the juice for making gravy. Leave the apricots to cool, then chop coarsely.

Heat the oven to 375°F, 190°C, Gas No. 5.

Melt the butter in a pan, add the onion and cook gently for about 10 minutes or until soft, but not brown, then stir in the apricots, breadcrumbs, nuts, lemon rind, sugar, parsley and plenty of seasoning. Mix thoroughly and use to stuff the neck end of the chicken.

Place the chicken in a roasting tin, cover the breast with a little butter and roast in the centre of the oven for about $1\frac{1}{2}$ hours or until tender. When the thickest part of the leg is pricked with a skewer the juices will run clear.

Serve with a gravy made using the apricot juice. Serves 6.

Don't chop the nuts too finely for this recipe. Brown breadcrumbs make a change from white and add to the flavour too.

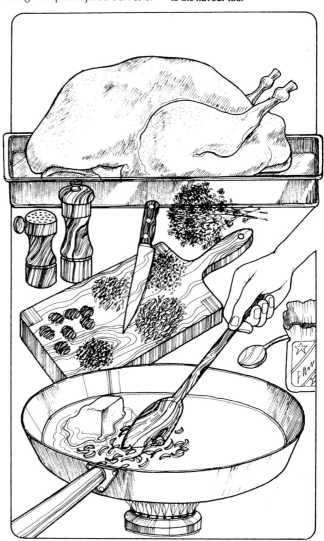

Mild chicken curry with cream and grapes

3 lb chicken
2 small onions, peeled
2 cloves
1 bayleaf
parsley
1 level teaspoon salt
6 peppercorns
½ pint water
½ pint sweet cider
¼ lb white grapes
1 oz butter
1 level teaspoon curry
    powder
1 oz flour
2 teaspoons redcurrant jelly
¼ pint single cream
salt and pepper
watercress

1.3 kg chicken
2 small onions, peeled
2 cloves
1 bayleaf
parsley
1 level teaspoon salt
6 peppercorns
300 ml water
300 ml sweet cider
100 gm white grapes
25 gm butter
1 level teaspoon curry
    powder
25 gm flour
2 teaspoons redcurrant jelly
150 ml single cream
salt and pepper
watercress

This has been a favourite of mine for years, and is perfect for a summer dinner party being light and mildly curry flavoured.

Place the chicken in a pan with the onions stuck with cloves, bayleaf, parsley, salt and peppercorns. Pour over the water and cider, cover the pan and simmer gently for 1 to 1¼ hours or until the chicken is tender.

While the chicken is cooking, skin and pip most of the grapes and put a few on one side for garnish.

Remove the chicken from the pan and leave to cool. Boil the stock rapidly until reduced to ½ pint (300 ml), strain and put on one side and skim off the surplus fat. Remove the flesh from the chicken, cut into neat pieces, place in a serving dish and keep warm.

Melt the butter in a pan, stir in the curry powder and cook gently for 2 minutes. Stir in the flour and cook for a minute. Slowly blend in the stock and bring to the boil, stirring. Add the redcurrant jelly and simmer for 2 to 3 minutes, season well and add the halved grapes.

Remove the sauce from the heat and stir in the cream. Coat the chicken with the sauce and garnish the dish with small sprigs of watercress and the remaining grapes.

Serve with boiled rice and a green salad. Serves 4 to 6.

Family meat dishes

French country casserole or pie

1 oz dripping
6 oz streaky bacon, rinded and cut in strips
1½ lb thin flank cut in 1 inch cubes
1 oz flour
½ pint stock
¼ pint red wine
1 bayleaf
sprig of parsley
good pinch mixed dried herbs or a small bunch of fresh herbs
1 level teaspoon salt
good pinch pepper
¼ lb small onions, peeled
7½ oz packet puff pastry, optional

25 gm dripping
175 gm streaky bacon, rinded and cut in strips
675 gm thin flank cut in 2.5 cm cubes
25 gm flour
300 ml stock
150 ml red wine
1 bayleaf
sprig of parsley
good pinch mixed dried herbs or a bunch of fresh herbs
1 level teaspoon salt
good pinch pepper
100 gm small onions, peeled
212 gm packet puff pastry, optional

Heat the oven to 325°F, 160°C, Gas No. 3. Melt the dripping in a frying pan and fry the bacon until it begins to brown. Lift out with a slotted spoon and place in a 3 pint (1.7 litre) oven-proof casserole. Fry the meat in the fat remaining in the pan until brown all over, lift out with the spoon and add to the bacon. Pour off all but 2 tablespoons of fat, stir in the flour and cook until browned. Add the stock and wine and bring to the boil, stirring all the time, then simmer for 2 minutes or until thickened. Add the bayleaf, parsley, herbs and seasoning and pour over the meat. Cover and cook in the oven for 1½ hours. Add the onions and cook for a further hour or until the meat is tender. Remove the parsley, bayleaf and bunch of herbs, taste and adjust seasoning. If making a pie, turn the mixture into a 1½ pint (1 litre) pie dish and leave to become quite cold. Roll out the pastry and use to cover the

An ideal opportunity to use an inexpensive cut of beef like thin flank, but remember to remove excess fat and skin first.

pie, re-roll any trimmings and cut into leaves to decorate the top. Make a small hole in the centre and brush with a little milk or beaten egg. Bake in a hot oven at 425°F, 220°C, Gas No. 7 for about 30 minutes until the pastry is golden brown and well risen and the meat is hot through. Serves 4 to 6 for the casserole or 6 to 8 for the pie.

Lamb hot pot

2 lb middle neck or scrag
   end of lamb or 1 lb neck
   fillet
2 lamb's kidneys
2 lb potatoes, sliced
2 onions, sliced
2 oz mushrooms, sliced
salt and pepper
about $\frac{1}{4}$ pint stock or water
butter

900 gm middle neck or
*   scrag end of lamb or*
*   450 gm neck fillet*
2 lamb's kidneys
900 gm potatoes, sliced
2 onions, sliced
50 gm mushrooms
salt and pepper
about 150 ml stock or water
butter

Heat the oven to 350°F, 180°C, Gas No. 4.

Trim the meat, removing the spinal cord and any excess fat, and cut into convenient sized pieces. Halve the kidneys and remove the core and skin, then cut into slices.

Layer the potato with the vegetables, lamb and kidneys in a large 4 to 5 pint (2.3 to 2.8 litre) casserole, seasoning well and finishing with a layer of potatoes arranged neatly on top.

Pour over the stock or water and dot the potatoes with a little butter. Cover and bake in the oven for 1 hour, remove the lid and continue baking for a further 30 to 45 minutes to brown the potatoes. Serves 4.

If your family can't cope with bones in their meat use 1 lb (450 gm) neck fillet of lamb. This is completely boneless, and you won't need such a large casserole.

Spicy beef cassoulet

4 oz dried red kidney beans	100 gm dried red kidney beans
2 good pinches bicarbonate of soda	2 good pinches bicarbonate of soda
1 oz flour	25 gm flour
1 teaspoon salt	1 teaspoon salt
good pinch pepper	good pinch pepper
2 good pinches ground ginger	2 good pinches ground ginger
1½ lb shin of beef cut in 1 inch cubes	675 gm shin of beef cut in 2.5 cm cubes
2 oz lard or dripping	50 gm lard or dripping
Sauce:	**Sauce:**
a few drops Tobasco sauce	a few drops Tobasco sauce
8 oz can peeled tomatoes	225 gm can peeled tomatoes
¼ pint stock	150 ml stock
2 tablespoons soft brown sugar	2 tablespoons soft brown sugar
¼ lb sliced mushrooms	100 gm sliced mushrooms
2 tablespoons cider vinegar	2 tablespoons cider vinegar
2 cloves garlic, crushed	2 cloves garlic, crushed
1 bayleaf	1 bayleaf
1 red pepper	1 red pepper

The red beans in this casserole must be soaked otherwise they are not soft enough to eat. The bicarbonate of soda speeds up the process but is not essential. If you are in a hurry use a 16 oz (450 gm) can of red kidney beans. This is an excellent dish for informal entertaining and delicious with a green salad.

Place the kidney beans in a basin with bicarbonate of soda, cover with cold water and leave to stand overnight; drain. Heat the oven to 325°F, 160°C, Gas No. 3. Mix the flour, seasoning and ginger together and coat the meat thoroughly; melt the dripping in a frying pan and fry the meat quickly to brown, then place in a 3 pint (1.7 litre) casserole with the beans. Combine all the sauce ingredients, except the red pepper, in the pan and bring to the boil. Pour this over the meat, cover and cook in the oven for about 2–3 hours.

Remove the seeds and white pith from the red pepper and cut into rings. Add to the casserole, return to the oven and cook for a further 30 minutes or until the beef is tender. Taste, adjust seasoning and remove the bayleaf. Serves 4 to 6.

Oxtail

1 oxtail, jointed, about
  $2\frac{1}{2}$ lb in weight
$1\frac{1}{2}$ oz dripping
1 oz flour
1 pint water
1 beef stock cube
2 onions, chopped
2 carrots, chopped
2 sticks celery, sliced
salt and pepper
pinch of cayenne pepper
1 bayleaf
a little gravy browning

*1 oxtail, jointed, about 1 kg
  in weight*
40 gm dripping
25 gm flour
600 ml water
1 beef stock cube
2 onions, chopped
2 carrots, chopped
2 sticks celery, sliced
salt and pepper
pinch cayenne pepper
1 bayleaf
a little gravy browning

Trim any excess fat from the oxtail. Heat the dripping in a large pan and fry the oxtail quickly on all sides to brown; remove from the pan. Stir the flour into the fat remaining in the pan and cook for a minute, then stir in the water and bring to the boil, add the stock cube and stir until dissolved.

Return the oxtail to the pan with the vegetables, seasoning and bay leaf, cover and simmer very gently for $3\frac{1}{2}$ to 4 hours until the meat can be easily removed from the bones. Skim off any surplus fat, remove the bayleaf.

Adjust the seasoning and add

Cook's Tip

Make sure to trim off excess fat from the joints. If the oxtail is cooked the day before it is required, leave it to cool completely before removing the fat.

a little gravy browning. Turn into a dish and serve. Serves 4 to 6.

19

Liver in onion sauce

1 lb pig's or lamb's liver
½ lb onions
2 oz dripping
2 oz flour
1 pint beef stock or 1 pint
   water and 1 beef stock
   cube
3 tablespoons tomato
   ketchup
pinch dried marjoram
a few drops of Worcester
   sauce
salt and pepper

450 gm pig's or lamb's liver
225 gm onions
50 gm dripping
50 gm flour
600 ml beef stock or 600 ml
   water and 1 beef stock
   cube
3 tablespoons tomato
   ketchup
pinch dried marjoram
a few drops of Worcester
   sauce
salt and pepper

If you don't like the stronger flavour of pig's liver but find lamb's liver too dear, then soak it in milk before cooking. This is a moist and flavoursome way of cooking it and your family will find it hard to tell the difference.

Cut the liver into long strips about ½ inch (1.25 cm) wide, then soak in milk for 30 minutes; drain off milk and discard.

Peel and slice the onions. Melt the dripping in a pan, add the onions and fry for 5 to 10 minutes until the onions are golden brown. Stir in the flour and cook for 2 minutes, add the stock and bring to the boil, stirring until thickened. Add ketchup, marjoram, Worcester sauce and seasoning, stir well and cover pan. Reduce heat and simmer for 20 minutes.

Add liver to sauce and cook for about 10 minutes. Serves 5.

Bacon-stuffed hearts

4 lamb's hearts
Stuffing:
$\frac{1}{4}$ lb streaky bacon
1 onion
3 oz cooked rice (1 oz raw rice)
1 level tablespoon chopped parsley
salt and pepper
Sauce:
10$\frac{1}{2}$ oz can condensed tomato soup
1 level tablespoon redcurrant jelly

4 lamb's hearts
Stuffing:
100 gm streaky bacon
1 onion
75 gm cooked rice (25 gm raw rice)
1 level teaspoon chopped parsley
salt and pepper
Sauce:
298 gm can condensed tomato soup
1 level tablespoon redcurrant jelly

Wash the hearts well and cut away the tubes.

Remove the rind and bone from the bacon and cut into strips. Peel and finely chop the onion and fry with the bacon for about 5 minutes so that the fat comes out of the bacon. Stir in the rice, parsley and seasoning. Divide the stuffing between the hearts, pressing firmly into the cavities, and secure with wooden cocktail sticks.

Place the hearts in a deep oven-proof casserole, pour over the soup and stir in the red-currant jelly. Cover with a lid or a piece of foil and bake in a moderate oven at 325°F, 160°C, Gas No. 3 for 1$\frac{3}{4}$ to 2 hours or until the hearts are tender. Remove the cocktail sticks before serving. Serves 4.

Rice is an ideal accompaniment to this dish and helps to sop up the delicious sauce.

Classic turkey roast

Thaw the turkey if frozen.

Check the weight of the bird with stuffing and calculate the cooking time. Preheat the oven.

Put a large piece of foil in the roasting tin. Lift turkey onto the foil and season well. Wrap the foil loosely over the bird with the fold at the top.

Put the turkey on a shelf just below the middle or lower in the oven according to the size of the bird.

To brown the turkey undo the foil and rub the breast and legs with butter. Cook with foil open for the last 1¼ hours of time for a large bird and about 50 minutes

for a small bird under 10 lbs (4.5 kg).

Put sausages in a greased roasting tin and cook above the turkey when the foil is opened. Add the bacon rolls on skewers on top of the sausages 30 minutes before the end of the cooking time.

Roast potatoes may be cooked for the last 1½ to 1¾ hours above the turkey. Bring pre-pared potatoes to the boil in a pan of water on the stove starting from cold. Drain. Heat oil or fat in a meat tin in the oven, then add potatoes. Turn during roasting.

When cooking a very large bird at a lower temperature, cook sausages, bacon and potatoes for a little longer.

6–7 lb (2.7 kg–3.2 kg) 3 to 3½ hours at 350°F, 180°C, Gas No. 4.
8–10 lb (3.6 kg–4.5 kg) 3½ to 4 hours at 350°F, 180°C, Gas No. 4.
11–15 lb (5.0 kg–6.9 kg) 4 to 4½ hours at 350°F, 180°C, Gas No. 4.
16–20 lb (7.2 kg–9.0 kg) 5 to 5½ hours at 325°F, 160°C, Gas No. 3.

Chestnut stuffing with watercress

1 lb 15 oz can whole
   chestnuts in water
8 oz streaky bacon,
   chopped
2 oz butter
4 oz fresh brown
   breadcrumbs
1 egg, beaten
1 bunch watercress, finely
   chopped
1 tablespoon castor sugar
2 teaspoons salt
ground black pepper

880 gm can whole chestnuts
   in water
225 gm streaky bacon,
   chopped
50 gm butter
100 gm fresh brown
   breadcrumbs
1 egg, beaten
1 bunch watercress, finely
   chopped
1 tablespoon castor sugar
2 teaspoons salt
ground black pepper

Drain the liquid from the chestnuts and turn them into a bowl. Gently mash with a fork to break into small chunky pieces.

Fry the bacon slowly to let the fat run out and then increase the heat and fry quickly until crisp. Lift out with a slotted spoon and add to the chestnuts.

Add the butter to the pan with the bacon fat and allow to melt, then add the breadcrumbs and fry until brown; turn into the bowl. Add the remaining ingredients and mix very thoroughly. Use to stuff the body cavity of the turkey.

These are two really good stuffings for turkey. Put the lemon, sausage and thyme stuffing in the breast end, but don't worry if it looks a big bulge: ease the skin a little to get all the stuffing in. Put the chestnut stuffing inside the body cavity of the bird.

Make the stuffings on Christmas Eve, wrap and put in the fridge and then stuff first thing on Christmas morning; the reason for not putting the stuffing in the bird the day before is that often there is not room to get the bird in the fridge because of all the other Christmas preparations. It is essential to refrigerate the stuffings so that they keep cold and fresh. The stuffings are enough for a **14 to 16 lb** bird (6.3 to 7.2 kg).

Sausage, lemon and thyme stuffing

1 oz butter
1 onion chopped
1 lb pork sausage meat
4 oz fresh white
   breadcrumbs
rind and juice of 1 lemon
1 level teaspoon salt
ground black pepper
2 tablespoons chopped
   parsley
1 level teaspoon fresh
   thyme or half teaspoon
   dried thyme

25 gm butter
1 onion chopped
450 gm pork sausage meat
100 gm fresh white
   breadcrumbs
rind and juice of 1 lemon
1 level teaspoon salt
ground black pepper
2 tablespoons chopped
   parsley
1 level teaspoon fresh thyme
   or half teaspoon dried
   thyme

Melt the butter, add the onion and fry gently until soft, for about 10 minutes. Stir in the remaining ingredients and mix well together. Use to stuff the breast of the turkey.

Vegetables

Chipped potatoes

old potatoes
oil for frying

Peel the potatoes and cut into $\frac{1}{4}$ to $\frac{1}{2}$ inch (5 mm to 1.25 cm) slices. Cut these slices into strips $\frac{1}{4}$ to $\frac{1}{2}$ inch (5 mm to 1.25 cm) wide. Wash in cold water, drain and dry thoroughly with a tea towel or on kitchen paper.

Heat the oil to 375°F, 190°C. To test whether the oil is hot enough, drop a chip into it. If it rises to the surface and bubbles, the oil is ready for frying.

Place a layer of chips in a wire basket and lower into the pan. Cook for about 4 minutes or until the chips are just cooked and a very pale golden brown. This is called blanching. Drain thoroughly on kitchen paper and repeat until all the chips have been fried.

Just before serving fry the chips again for a few minutes until golden brown. Drain well and serve, sprinkling with a little salt if liked.

To freeze chips: deep-fat fry the chips in hot oil, 360°F, 185°C, or until just tender but not browned. Drain thoroughly on kitchen paper and cool quickly.

The best potatoes for making chips are Maris Piper main crop potatoes. These are the ones that the best British fish and chip shops use.

Open-freeze then pack into polythene bags, seal, label and return to the freezer. The frying temperature is lower as the chipped potatoes are not browned for freezing. Thaw the chips, turn into hot oil and cook until golden brown. Drain well before serving.

French vegetable quiche

6 oz plain flour
4 oz butter
1½ oz Parmesan cheese
1 tablespoon cold water
1 egg yolk
Filling:
1 oz butter
1 oz flour
½ pint milk
1 level teaspoon made
   mustard
3 oz grated Cheddar cheese
salt and pepper
¾ lb cooked mixed
   vegetables (e.g. leeks,
   carrots, peas, beans; not
   cabbage or sprouts)
chopped parsley

175 gm plain flour
100 gm butter
40 gm Parmesan cheese
15 ml cold water
1 egg yolk
Filling:
25 gm butter
25 gm flour
300 ml milk
1 level teaspoon made
   mustard
75 gm grated Cheddar
salt and pepper
350 gm cooked mixed
   vegetables (e.g. leeks,
   carrots, peas, beans; not
   cabbage or sprouts)
chopped parsley

Cook's Tip

This makes a very good family supper dish and is an excellent way of using up a selection of leftover vegetables, as long as they are barely tender. Make the flan case in advance and warm it through in the oven to crispen the pastry before filling with the vegetables and sauce. For extra hungry guests you could add chopped cooked ham or garnish the flan with bacon rolls.

Sift the flour into a bowl. Add the butter cut in small pieces and rub in with the fingertips until the mixture resembles fine breadcrumbs. Stir in the Parmesan cheese. Blend the water with the egg yolk, add to the flour and mix to a firm dough. Roll out on a lightly floured table and line an 9 inch (22.5 cm) flan tin. Chill in the refrigerator for 15 minutes.

Heat the oven to 425°F, 220°C, Gas No. 7. Put in a baking sheet to warm. Line the flan with a piece of greaseproof paper and weigh down with baking beans. Bake blind for 20 to 25 minutes until pastry is golden brown at the edges and crisp.

Meanwhile melt the butter for the filling in a saucepan and stir in the flour. Cook for 2 minutes. Gradually add the milk and bring to the boil, stirring until thickened. Add the mustard, cheese and seasoning.

Cut the vegetables into even sized pieces and add to the sauce. Re-heat thoroughly and then spoon into the flan case. Sprinkle with parsley and serve. Serves 6.

Ratatouille

1 green pepper
1 red pepper
4 tablespoons oil
2 Spanish onions, sliced
2 courgettes, sliced
8 oz tomatoes, skinned,
   quartered and the seeds
   removed
salt and pepper

1 green pepper
1 red pepper
4 tablespoons oil
2 Spanish onions, sliced
2 courgettes, sliced
225 gm tomatoes, skinned,
   quartered and the seeds
   removed
salt and pepper

Remove the seeds and pith from the green and red peppers and cut into strips. Heat the oil in a thick pan and add the peppers and onions, cover and cook slowly for about 20 minutes, stirring occasionally until the onions are soft.

Add the courgettes and tomatoes with plenty of salt and pepper and cook without the lid for a further 10 to 15 minutes or until the courgettes are tender. Taste and check seasoning and serve piping hot. Serves 4.

Make ratatouille when peppers and courgettes are reasonably priced in the summer. Add garlic as well if you like it. Serve with meat without a sauce such as a roast chicken or grilled fish or chops.

Nicoise salad

4 firm tomatoes
½ cucumber
8 oz French beans, cooked
   until crisp
2 spring onions, chopped
1 cos or Webb's lettuce
⅛ pint French dressing
2 oz can anchovy fillets
7 oz can tuna
3 hard-boiled eggs
2 tablespoons coarsely
   chopped parsley

4 firm tomatoes
½ cucumber
225 gm French beans,
   cooked until crisp
2 spring onions, chopped
1 cos or Webb's lettuce
75 ml French dressing
50 gm anchovy fillets
200 gm can tuna
3 hard-boiled eggs
2 tablespoons coarsely
   chopped parsley

Cos or Webb's lettuce are perfect for this. Don't use a flabby round lettuce as it does not have the crispness.

Quarter the tomatoes, slice the cucumber, cut the French beans into short lengths and add to the spring onions.

Wash the lettuce, tear into strips and arrange in the bottom of the salad bowl. Thoroughly drain the anchovy fillets and add with the vegetables to the French dressing, toss lightly and spoon over the lettuce.

Drain the tuna fish, lightly flake and place on top of the vegetables. Cut each egg in half lengthwise and arrange around the edge of the salad, sprinkle with parsley and serve. If liked the salad may be tossed lightly to mix all the ingredients together but take care not to over blend or the appearance will be messy. Serves 6.

Swedish salad platter

Curried egg mayonnaise

Halve two hard-boiled eggs lengthwise and lay cut-side down along the edge of a large serving dish. Blend a little mayonnaise with a good pinch of curry powder, squeeze of lemon juice and a little mango chutney juice and spoon over the eggs. Sprinkle each egg with paprika pepper.

Cucumber and dill

Toss slices of peeled cucumber in a little French dressing that has had some chopped fresh dill tips added to it and spoon in a line onto the dish alongside the egg mayonnaise. Decorate with dill.

Ham rolls

Finely dice a large cooked potato and mix with 2 sticks sliced celery and a chopped eating apple. Add just sufficient mayonnaise to bind well together. Place a spoonful of the mixture on each of the 4 slices of ham and roll up. Place in a line on the dish alongside the cucumber and dill salad.

This is a colourful salad dish which may be served as an hors d'oeuvre. It also makes an attractive addition to any buffet meal. Serves 4.

Tomato and onion

Peel and slice 8 oz (225 gm) tomatoes and mix with a very finely sliced onion. Lightly toss in a little French dressing and spoon onto the plate alongside the rolls. Sprinkle with a few finely chopped chives.

Hot puddings

Soufflé omelette

2 large eggs
1 dessertspoon castor
   sugar
2 teaspoons cold water
½ oz butter
1 rounded tablespoon
   strawberry or black
   cherry jam
icing sugar

2 large eggs
1 dessertspoon castor
   sugar
2 teaspoons cold water
12.5 gm butter
1 rounded tablespoon
   strawberry or black
   cherry jam
icing sugar

This is an easy pudding that can quickly be made out of ingredients that most of us have to hand.

Separate the eggs and place the yolks in a basin with the sugar and water, beat until pale and creamy.

Whisk the egg whites using a hand rotary or electric whisk until just stiff. Mix 1 tablespoonful into the yolks and carefully fold in the remainder.

Heat the pan and then melt the butter in it over a moderate heat. Spread the mixture into the pan and cook without moving for 3 to 4 minutes until a pale golden brown underneath.

Slip under a medium grill for 2 to 3 minutes to set the

top. Make a slight cut across the centre of the omelette, spread one half with warmed jam, fold in half and slide on to a warm serving plate. Dredge with icing sugar and serve at once. Serves 2.

Christmas pudding

2 oz self-raising flour
good pinch mixed spice
good pinch grated nutmeg
good pinch salt
4 oz currants
4 oz sultanas
4 oz stoned raisins
3 oz fresh white
    breadcrumbs
3 oz shredded suet
1 oz chopped mixed peel
1 oz almonds, blanched
1 small cooking apple
1 rounded tablespoon
    marmalade
3 oz grated carrot
4 oz soft brown sugar
2 eggs

50 gm self-raising flour
good pinch mixed spice
good pinch grated nutmeg
good pinch salt
100 gm currants
100 gm sultanas
100 gm stoned raisins
75 gm fresh white
    breadcrumbs
75 gm shredded suet
25 gm chopped mixed peel
25 gm almonds, blanched
1 small cooking apple
1 rounded tablespoon
    marmalade
75 gm grated carrot
100 gm soft brown sugar
2 eggs

Grease a 1½ pint (900 ml) pudding basin.

Sift together the flour, spices and salt. Put the currants and sultanas in a large bowl, roughly chop the raisins and add with the breadcrumbs, suet and peel.

Roughly chop the almonds. Peel the apple and coarsely grate, add to the bowl with the almonds, marmalade and carrot. Stir in the spiced flour and sugar. Mix well together. Lightly beat the eggs and stir into the mixture.

Turn into the greased basin, cover the top with greaseproof paper and a foil lid. Simmer gently for 6 hours. Lift out of the pan, leaving the greaseproof and foil in place. Cool, cover with a fresh foil lid and store.

Simmer for 3 hours on Christmas day. Serves 8.

When the pudding is cooked, cool and then cover with a new piece of foil. Store in a cool place until Christmas day then boil for a further 3 hours or so.

Chocolate soufflé

4 oz plain chocolate
2 tablespoons water
$\frac{1}{2}$ pint milk
1$\frac{1}{2}$ oz butter
1$\frac{1}{2}$ oz flour
1 teaspoon vanilla essence
4 large eggs
2 oz castor sugar
a little icing sugar

100 gm plain chocolate
2 tablespoons water
300 ml milk
40 gm butter
40 gm flour
1 teaspoon vanilla essence
4 large eggs
50 gm castor sugar
a little icing sugar

Heat the oven to 375°F, 190°C, Gas No. 5 and place a baking sheet in it.

Cut the chocolate into small pieces, put in a pan with the water and 2 tablespoons milk.

Stir over a low heat until the chocolate has melted. Add the remaining milk, bring to the boil and remove from the heat.

Melt the butter in a small pan, stir in the flour and cook for 2 minutes without browning. Remove from the heat and stir in the hot milk, return to the heat and bring to the boil, stirring until thickened. Add the vanilla essence and leave to cool.

Separate the eggs and beat the yolks one at a time into the chocolate sauce. Sprinkle on the sugar. Whisk the egg whites using a rotary hand whisk or an electric whisk until stiff but not dry. Stir one tablespoonful into the mixture then carefully fold in the remainder. Pour into a buttered 2 pint (good 1 litre) soufflé dish, run a teaspoon around the edge and bake on the hot baking sheet in the centre of the oven for about 40 minutes. Sprinkle with icing sugar and serve at once with

So good and not one bit difficult to make as long as you have a rotary whisk or an electric beater to whisk the egg whites. Make sure you use the correct size dish because if you choose a larger one the mixture will not rise above the rim. Serve with whipped cream.

whipped cream. Serves 4.

Variations

Choose any flavouring and add to the mixture before the egg yolks.

Lemon: Add the finely grated rind of 2 small lemons and the juice of $\frac{1}{2}$ a lemon and increase the sugar to 3 oz (75 gm).

Orange: Add the finely grated rind of 2 small oranges and the juice of $\frac{1}{2}$ an orange and increase the sugar to 3 oz (75 gm).

Coffee: Add 2 tablespoons coffee essence to the milk.

Lemon soufflé pudding

4 oz butter or margarine, softened
12 oz castor sugar
4 eggs, separated
4 oz self-raising flour
grated rind of 2 large lemons
6 tablespoons lemon juice
1 pint milk

100 gm butter or margarine softened
350 gm castor sugar
4 eggs separated
100 gm self-raising flour
grated rind of 2 large lemons
6 tablespoons lemon juice
600 ml milk

Heat the oven to 375°F, 190°C, Gas No. 5. Butter well a shallow 3 pint (1.5 litre) ovenproof dish.

Beat the butter or margarine with the sugar until smooth. Beat in the egg yolks, then stir in the flour, lemon rind, juice and milk. Don't worry if the mixture looks curdled at this stage; it is quite normal.

Whisk the egg whites using a hand rotary or electric whisk until they form soft peaks and fold into the lemon mixture. Pour into the prepared dish and place in a meat tin half filled with hot water. Bake for about 1 hour or until pale golden brown on top. The pudding will have a light sponge on top with its own lemon sauce underneath. Serves 4 hungry people or 6 average helpings.

This lemon pudding has something to please everyone, for it combines a hot lemon soufflé with its own built-in sauce.

Mince pie

8 oz plain flour
generous pinch salt
3 oz margarine, chilled and cut in ½ inch cubes
3 oz lard, chilled and cut in ½ inch cubes
about ¼ pint cold water
1 lb jar of mincemeat
milk
castor sugar

225 gm plain flour
generous pinch salt
75 gm margarine, chilled and cut in 1.25 cm cubes
75 gm lard, chilled and cut in 1.25 cm cubes
about 150 ml cold water
450 gm jar of mincemeat
milk
castor sugar

Making one large pie means that you have lots of filling and not too much pastry. Use a cheaper hard margarine for the pastry rather than one of the soft more expensive kinds. Delicious served warm with cream or brandy butter.

Sift the flour and salt into a mixing bowl. Add the cubes of margarine and lard and just enough cold water to mix to a firm pastry, using a sharp knife. On a lightly floured surface roll out the pastry to a strip ½ inch (1.25 cm) thick and 6 inches (15 cm) wide. Fold pastry in 3 and give it a quarter turn to the left. Roll out again into a strip and fold in 3. Wrap the pastry in greaseproof paper and chill in the refrigerator for 30 minutes.

Divide the pastry into 2 portions, one slightly larger than the other. Roll out smaller portion to a ¼ inch (5 mm) thick circle and use it to line an 10 inch (25 cm) pie plate (preferably made of enamel, tin or foil). Spoon the mincemeat into the dish.

Roll out the remaining pastry to a circle ¼ inch (5 mm) thick. Brush the edges of the pastry already on the pie plate with milk and cover the mincemeat filling with the second pastry circle. Press edges together to seal, trim off excess pastry and crimp edges to make a decorative finish. Place in the refrigerator to chill for 10 minutes.

Brush the top of the pie with milk and place in the oven preheated to 425°F, 220°C, Gas No. 7. Bake for 25 minutes or until the pastry is golden brown. Sprinkle with castor sugar and serve warm. Serves 8.

Cold puddings

Pavlova

3 egg whites
6 oz castor sugar
1 teaspoon vinegar
1 level teaspoon cornflour
½ pint whipped whipping
cream
8 oz frozen raspberries,
just thawed
a little castor sugar to
sweeten

3 egg whites
175 gm castor sugar
1 teaspoon vinegar
1 level teaspoon cornflour
300 ml whipped whipping
cream
225 gm frozen raspberries,
just thawed
a little castor sugar to
sweeten

Lay a sheet of silicone paper (non-stick vegetable parchment) on a baking tray and mark an 8 inch (20 cm) circle on it. Heat the oven to 325°F, 160°C, Gas No. 3.

Whisk the egg whites with a hand rotary or electric whisk until stiff, then whisk in the sugar a spoonful at a time. Blend the vinegar with the cornflour and whisk into the egg whites with the last spoonful of sugar.

Spread the meringue out to cover the circle on the baking tray, building up the sides so that they are higher than the centre.

Put in the centre of the oven, turn the heat down to 300°F, 150°C, Gas No. 2 and bake for 1 hour. The pavlova will be a pale creamy colour rather than white. Turn the oven off and leave the pavlova to become quite cold in the oven.

Remove from the baking tray and place on a serving dish.

Fold the cream and raspberries together lightly and sweeten to taste. Pile into the centre of the pavlova and leave to stand for an hour in the refrigerator before serving. Serves 6.

Chocolate and orange mousse

½ oz gelatine
1 tablespoon water
rind and juice of 1 orange
8 oz plain chocolate
5 eggs, separated
4 oz castor sugar
½ pint whipping cream,
    whipped

12.5 gm gelatine
1 tablespoon water
rind and juice of 1 orange
225 gm plain chocolate
5 eggs, separated
100 gm castor sugar
300 ml whipping cream,
    whipped

Soak the gelatine in the water with the rind and juice of the orange in a small cup or basin and leave until it becomes spongy. Then stand in a pan of simmering water until it has completely dissolved and is runny.

Put another basin containing the chocolate broken into small pieces over the pan of hot water and leave until melted. Add the 5 egg yolks and stir until smooth.

Pour the gelatine into a small mixing bowl and stir in the chocolate mixture and leave for about 5 minutes until cool but not set.

Meanwhile whisk the egg whites using a hand electric or rotary whisk until frothy then add the sugar a teaspoonful

This is sinfully rich and takes time to make but it is well worth it for a special occasion.

at a time whisking all the time until you have the consistency of a meringue. Quickly fold in the chocolate, yolk, orange and gelatine mixture then fold in half the whipped cream. Turn into individual glass dishes, cover with cling film and chill until set. Then decorate with chocolate and swirls of the remaining whipped cream. Serves 6 to 8.

Rosy red fruit salad

1 large orange
4 cloves
1 lb blackcurrants
$\frac{1}{2}$ lb blackberries
6 oz granulated sugar
$\frac{1}{4}$ pint water
8 oz raspberries
1 lb fresh pears, peeled,
    cored and sliced

1 large orange
4 cloves
450 gm blackcurrants
225 gm blackberries
175 gm granulated sugar
150 ml water
225 gm raspberries
450 gm fresh pears, peeled,
    cored and sliced

Cut strips of peel from the orange, stick in the cloves and place in a saucepan with the blackcurrants, blackberries, sugar and water, cover and simmer gently for 10 minutes or until tender.

Turn into a bowl, remove and discard the orange peel, cut the orange into segments. Leave to cool, then chill thoroughly.

Stir in the raspberries, pears and orange just before serving. Serves 6.

This uses mostly frozen fruit and is especially good served with lightly whipped cream or ice cream.

Apple jelly with grapes

To turn out a jelly, first dip the mould quickly into very hot water. Put a plate on top of it and turn sharply upside down. If you have previously wetted the plate you will be able to slide the jelly into a central position should it not land in the middle of the plate. The apple juice can be replaced with cider: both are good. Serve the jelly chilled.

1 packet lime jelly
$\frac{1}{4}$ pint boiling water
$\frac{1}{2}$ pint apple juice
8 oz large green grapes

1 packet lime jelly
150 ml boiling water
300 ml apple juice
225 gm large green grapes

Dissolve the jelly in the boiling water. Stir in the apple juice.

Halve the grapes and remove all the pips.

Pour $\frac{1}{3}$ of the liquid into the jelly mould and stir in the grapes. Leave to set in the refrigerator, then pour in the remaining jelly. Should this have started to set, heat it slightly so that it melts before pouring it into the mould. Leave until set and thoroughly chill before turning out and serving. Serves 4.

Quick lemon mousse

4 eggs
4 oz castor sugar
2 large lemons
$\frac{1}{2}$ oz gelatine
3 tablespoons cold water
whipped cream and lemon
   slices to decorate

4 eggs
100 gm castor sugar
2 large lemons
12.5 gm gelatine
3 tablespoons cold water
whipped cream and lemon
   slices to decorate

Separate the eggs, place the yolks in a bowl with the sugar and beat until well blended and creamy. Put the whites in a bowl ready for whisking.

Grate the rind and squeeze the juice from the lemons and add both to the yolk mixture.

Place the gelatine and water in a small bowl or cup. Leave for 3 minutes until thick, then stand the bowl in a pan of simmering water and allow the gelatine to dissolve. Cool slightly and add to the yolk and lemon mixture; leave to cool but not set.

Whisk the egg whites, using a rotary or electric whisk until stiff, then fold into the lemon mixture. Put into a 2 pint (1 litre) glass dish and chill for at least 4 hours to set.

Decorate with whipped cream and lemon slices and serve at room temperature. Serves 6.

A very simple sharp mousse. I find it popular after a large meal especially at Christmas time.

Blackberry mousse

1 lb blackberries
4 oz castor sugar
juice of 1 small lemon
3 tablespoons cold water
½ oz gelatine
¼ pint double cream
2 egg whites

450 gm blackberries
100 gm castor sugar
juice of 1 small lemon
3 tablespoons cold water
12.5 gm gelatine
150 ml double cream
2 egg whites

Blackberries will give a superb strong flavour to mousses and team deliciously with apples in pies or crumbles. The best thing about them is that they are free, so make as much use of them as you can, while they last.

Wash and pick over the blackberries and put in a saucepan with the sugar and lemon juice. Place over a low heat and simmer gently for about 10 minutes with the lid on until the blackberries are soft and the juice is running out.

Put the water in a small bowl or cup and sprinkle over the gelatine. Soak for 5 minutes.

Take the fruit from the heat and stir in the soaked gelatine until it has dissolved. Sieve the fruit into a large bowl to make a puree and leave on one side until beginning to thicken and quite cold.

Lightly whisk all but one tablespoon of the cream and whisk the egg whites with a hand or electric whisk until stiff. Fold the whisked cream and egg whites into the puree until blended and turn into a 2 pint (1 litre) glass serving dish. Swirl the last spoonful of cream into the centre of the mousse and leave in a cool place until set. Serves 6.

Gooseberry fool

1 lb gooseberries
2 tablespoons water
3 to 4 oz castor sugar
17 fl oz family brick vanilla
   ice cream
a little green colouring

450 gm gooseberries,
2 tablespoons water
75 to 100 gm castor sugar
510 ml family brick vanilla
   ice cream
a little green colouring

An ideal pudding if you're in a hurry; being tart and light it is often welcome after a heavy or rich meal.

Place the gooseberries in a saucepan with the water, cover and cook gently until tender for about 15 to 20 minutes. Remove from the heat and sieve into a bowl, add sugar to taste and leave the puree to become quite cold.

Remove the ice cream from the freezer and leave to soften at room temperature for about 10 to 15 minutes. Stir the ice cream into the puree and mix until well blended. If liked add a little green colouring.

Turn into a dish and serve with brandy snaps. Serves 4.

Quick lemon cheesecake

¼ pint boiling water
1 lemon jelly
juice of 2 lemons and the
   rind of 1 lemon
12 oz rich cream cheese
¼ pint double cream
3 to 4 oz castor sugar
2 oz digestive biscuits,
   crushed
2 oz ginger biscuits,
   crushed
1 oz demerara sugar
2 oz butter, melted
a little soured cream
lemon slices

150 ml boiling water
1 lemon jelly
juice of 2 lemons and the
   rind of 1 lemon
350 gm rich cream cheese
150 ml double cream
75 to 100 gm castor sugar
50 gm digestive biscuits,
   crushed
50 gm ginger biscuits,
   crushed
25 gm demerara sugar
50 gm butter, melted
a little soured cream
lemon slices

The crust of this cheesecake needs explaining: it is put on top of the cheesecake when in the cake tin so that when you reverse the tin to turn it out onto a flat plate the crust is underneath.

Put the boiling water in a measuring jug with the jelly and stir until dissolved. Add the lemon rind and juice and if necessary make up to ½ pint (300 ml) with extra cold water. Leave to become quite cold and nearly set.

Mix the cream cheese with a little of the cream and whisk the remainder until it forms soft peaks; fold into cheese with castor sugar and almost-set jelly mixture. Turn into an 8 inch (20 cm) cake tin lined with a circle of greaseproof paper and chill in the refrigerator until set.

Mix together the crushed biscuits, sugar and melted butter and spread over the cheesecake; chill for a further hour.

Dip tin into very hot water for a brief moment to loosen cheesecake, then turn out onto a serving dish, remove the circle of greaseproof paper and spread the top with soured cream. Before serving decorate with lemon slices. Serves 8.

Thomas's flan

Flan case:
2 oz butter or margarine
1 level tablespoon sugar
8 digestive biscuits, crushed
Filling:
6 oz can condensed milk
¼ pint double cream
juice of 2 lemons
halved grapes to decorate

Flan case:
50 gm butter or margarine
1 level tablespoon sugar
8 digestive biscuits, crushed
Filling:
175 gm can condensed milk
150 ml double cream
juice of 2 lemons
halved grapes to decorate

This is a flan so easy to make that it is ideal for children's cooking. It is named after my elder son who makes it regularly. Delicious after a Sunday roast.

Melt the butter or margarine in a saucepan, remove from the heat and stir in the sugar and crushed biscuits. Mix well and press the mixture over the base and sides of a 7 inch (17.5cm) flan ring or loose-bottomed flan tin. Spread evenly using a metal tablespoon.

Put the condensed milk, cream and lemon juice in a bowl and whisk the mixture together until well blended. Pour into the flan case.

Chill for at least 4 hours in the refrigerator. Before serving remove the flan ring and decorate with halved grapes. Serves 4–6.

Ice cream

Lemon ice cream

4 eggs, separated
4 oz castor sugar
½ pint double cream
grated rind and juice of
    2 lemons

4 eggs, separated
100 gm castor sugar
300 ml double cream
grated rind and juice of
    2 lemons

A quick easy ice cream with a sharp lemon flavour. No need to whip the ice cream half way through freezing as it is beautifully creamy without.

Whisk the yolks in a small bowl until blended. In a larger bowl whisk the egg whites with a hand rotary or electric whisk until stiff, then whisk in the sugar a teaspoonful at a time.

Whisk the cream with the lemon rind and juice until it forms soft peaks and then fold into the meringue mixture with the egg yolks.

Turn into a 2½ pint (1.4 litre)

container, cover, label and freeze.

Leave to thaw at room temperature for 5 minutes then serve in scoops in small glasses or dishes. Serves 6 to 8.

Praline ice cream

1½ oz whole blanched
    almonds
5½ oz castor sugar
4 eggs
½ pint whipping cream

40 gm whole blanched
    almonds
162.5 gm castor sugar
4 eggs
300 ml whipping cream

This ice cream is delicious served with brandy snaps because of the unexpected crunchy pieces of caramel it contains.

Put the almonds with 1½ oz (40 gm) castor sugar in a heavy pan and place over a low heat, stirring occasionally until the sugar has melted and is beginning to caramelize. This will take about 15 minutes. Continue to cook until the mixture is an even golden brown and the nuts are glazed. Remove from the heat and pour onto an oiled enamel plate or baking tray. Leave until quite firm and

cold. Turn into a grinder or blender and grind coarsely or crush with a rolling pin.

Separate the eggs, place the yolks in a small bowl and whisk until well blended. In another larger bowl whisk the egg whites until stiff and then whisk in the remaining castor sugar a spoonful at a time. Whisk the cream until it forms soft peaks and fold into the meringue mixture with the egg yolks and praline.

Turn into a 2½ pint (1.5 litre) rigid container, cover, label and freeze.

Remove from the refrigerator and leave to stand for 5 minutes. Serve in scoops in individual glasses with brandy snaps. Serves 6 to 8.

▶ *(P. 44/45) Melon with mint sorbet, Lemon ice cream and Praline ice cream*

Melon mint sorbet

scant ¾ pint water
6 oz castor sugar
rind and juice of 2 lemons
2 egg whites, lightly
  whipped
half an Ogen or Galia melon
leaves of 6 young sprigs
  of mint

scant 450 ml water
175 gm castor sugar
rind and juice of 2 lemons
2 egg whites, lightly whipped
*half an Ogen or Galia
  melon*
*leaves of 6 young sprigs of
  mint*

**A delicious refreshing sweet to
serve after a heavy main course.**

Put the water and sugar in a saucepan and stir over low heat until the sugar has dissolved. Add the thinly pared rind of the lemons; use a vegetable peeler and pare off only the fine outer yellow zest. Bring to the boil and then boil rapidly for 5 minutes, draw off the heat, strain into a bowl and leave to cool.

Add the strained lemon juice and lightly whipped egg whites.

Remove the seeds from the melon and scoop out the fruit from the skin. Place the melon in a blender with the mint leaves and puree until smooth. Stir into the lemon mixture, pour into a rigid plastic container, cover and freeze for about 3 hours until the mixture is mushy.

Spoon the partially frozen mixture into a large bowl and whisk until smooth and white.

Return the mixture to the container, cover, label and freeze. Put the melon shell in a plastic bag and freeze too. When required, serve the sorbet in scoops in the melon shell. Serves 8.

Cakes and baking

Marmalade fruitcake

6 oz soft margarine
6 oz soft brown sugar
12 oz mixed dried fruit
3 large eggs, beaten
9 oz self-raising flour
2 oz glacé cherries,
    quartered
2 level tablespoons
    chopped chunky
    marmalade

175 gm soft margarine
175 gm soft brown sugar
350 gm mixed dried fruit
3 large eggs, beaten
250 gm self-raising flour
50 gm glacé cherries,
    quartered
2 level tablespoons
    chopped chunky
    marmalade

Heat the oven to 325°F, 160°C, Gas No. 3. Grease and line an 8 inch (20 cm) round cake tin with greased greaseproof paper.

Put all the ingredients together in a bowl and mix well until blended. Turn into the tin and spread evenly leaving a slight hollow in the top. Bake just above the centre of the oven for about $2\frac{1}{4}$ hours; when the cake is pierced with a skewer in the centre it will come out clean. Leave to cool in the tin for 10 minutes, then turn out onto a wire rack and leave until cold.

A first-rate family fruit cake, but don't overdo the marmalade otherwise the fruit will sink to the bottom.

Traditional Christmas cake

Make this one up to a couple of months before Christmas and keep in a tin. Add the almond paste about 10 days before Christmas, then leave to dry out for 5 to 6 days before covering with royal icing.

12 oz seedless raisins	350 gm seedless raisins
12 oz sultanas	350 gm sultanas
12 oz currants	350 gm currants
2 oz cut mixed peel	50 gm cut mixed peel
4 oz glacé cherries, halved	100 gm glacé cherries, halved
grated rind and juice of 1 lemon	grated rind and juice of 1 lemon
2 oz blanched almonds, chopped	50 gm blanched almonds, chopped
9 oz plain flour	250 gm plain flour
good pinch salt	good pinch salt
1 teaspoon mixed spice	1 teaspoon mixed spice
8 oz butter	225 gm butter
8 oz soft brown sugar	225 gm soft brown sugar
4 eggs, beaten	4 eggs, beaten
1 tablespoon black treacle	1 tablespoon black treacle
2 tablespoons brandy	2 tablespoons brandy

Heat the oven to 300°F, 150°C, Gas No. 2. Grease and line with a double thickness of greased greaseproof paper a deep 8 inch (20cm) round cake tin.

In a bowl mix the dried fruit with the peel, cherries, grated lemon rind and almonds. Sift the flour, salt and spice onto a plate.

In a large bowl cream the butter and sugar until soft and fluffy. Beat in the eggs adding 1 tablespoon flour with each egg. Fold in the remaining flour with the fruit, lemon juice, treacle and brandy.

Turn into the cake tin and smooth the top, leaving a slight hollow in the centre. Bake in the oven for about 3–3½ hours or until cooked and pale golden brown. To test, gently prick with a fine skewer: If it comes out clean, the cake is ready. Leave to cool in the tin, then store in an airtight tin.

Christmas cake with pineapple

2 oz glacé cherries
7 oz self-raising flour
8 oz can pineapple in
   chunks, rings or crushed,
   excluding all the juice
5 oz butter
4½ oz soft brown sugar
2 large eggs, beaten
2 tablespoons milk
12 oz mixed dried fruit

50 gm glacé cherries
200 gm self-raising flour
225 gm can pineapple in
   chunks, rings or crushed,
   excluding all the juice
150 gm butter
112 gm soft brown sugar
2 large eggs, beaten
2 tablespoons milk
350 gm mixed dried fruit

This is a really moist, less-rich Christmas cake. It can be made just before Christmas and is best kept fairly cool and used within a month. The pineapple gives a good flavour. Make sure to drain it well and use the juice in a fruit salad or trifle.

Grease an 8 inch (20 cm) round cake tin and line with greased greaseproof paper. Cut cherries in halves and roll in flour. Drain and chop the pineapple very finely.

Cream the butter and sugar together in a mixing bowl. Beat in the eggs, adding a tablespoon of flour with the last amount of egg. Fold in flour, milk and last of all the fruit

including the pineapple.

Turn into the prepared tin and place in the centre of the oven preheated to 325°F, 160°C, Gas No. 3 and bake for about 2 hours until pale golden brown and shrinking away from the sides of the tin.

Leave to cool in the tin, remove the paper and store in a plastic container in the refrigerator.

Almond paste

6 oz icing sugar
6 oz ground almonds
6 oz castor sugar
3 egg yolks
almond essence
juice of half a lemon

175 gm icing sugar
175 gm ground almonds
175 gm castor sugar
3 egg yolks
almond essence
juice of half a lemon

This is enough for icing the sides and top of an 8 inch (20 cm) round cake.

Sift the icing sugar into a bowl. Add the ground almonds and castor sugar and mix well.

Add the lightly beaten egg yolks, flavour with almond essence and add the lemon juice. Work the mixture into a small smooth ball by hand and do not over knead.

To cover with almond paste

Divide the almond paste into 2 pieces, in proportion two thirds to one third. Cut out paper patterns of a circle to fit the top of the cake and strip to fit round the side. Lay these out on a table and sugar them with a little castor sugar. Roll out the smaller piece of almond paste to fit the circle and the larger to fit the strip generously. For the sides, it helps to roll a long sausage shape of almond paste, and then flatten it.

Put the top in position leaving the paper on, and turn the cake over. Brush side of cake with jam. Fix the strip of almond paste to the side and remove paper. Neaten the edges with a palette knife and roll a straight-sided tin around the cake to make the side smooth. Turn the cake back the right way up and put on a board. Level the top with a rolling pin.

Cover cake and leave in a cool airy place for 5 to 6 days.

Royal icing

1½ lb icing sugar
4 egg whites
3 teaspoons lemon juice
1½ teaspoons glycerine

675 gm icing sugar
4 egg whites
3 teaspoons lemon juice
1½ teaspoons glycerine

This is enough for the top and sides of an 8 inch (20 cm) round cake. I suggest that you make the sides peaky and rough which looks Christmassy and is easier.

Sieve the icing sugar. Whisk 3 egg whites in a bowl until they become frothy. Add the icing sugar a spoonful at a time, then add the lemon juice and glycerine. Beat the icing until it is very white and stiff enough to stand up in peaks.

To ice the cake
Set the cake on a 10 inch (25 cm) cake board.

Make a thin round base 4 inches (10 cm) across from cardboard and foil to go under the decorations.

Christmas roses

Roses:
small teacup royal icing
coffee spoon tragacanth
  (from chemists)
yellow and green vegetable
  colouring

Holly:
trimmings of almond paste

These are tricky to make but worth the trouble if you want your Christmas cake to look extra special. They are meant to be kept and not eaten!

Sprinkle the tragacanth over the royal icing and stir until a stiff paste. Mould five small thin petals for each flower and arrange over the top of a foil-covered capped bottle, over-lapping the petals and sticking them together with egg white. Allow the petals to fall naturally to resemble a Christmas rose, leave to set.

Reverse each flower in a small cup of foil while making the next flower. When you have made 5 flowers roll out the rest of the icing paste into a strip $\frac{1}{2} \times 6$ inches (1.25 × 15 cm) and snip with scissors all along the 6 inch (15 cm) sides. Divide into 5 pieces and roll up each piece to make stamens for the flowers. Fix in the centre and paint yellow with a little colouring.

Make leaves by colouring almond paste green, rolling out thinly and cutting diamond shapes from the paste. To form points of holly leaves use $\frac{1}{4}$ inch (6 mm) cutter or cap of ball point pen and cut around each diamond shape. Lay each leaf over the handle of a wooden spoon to form an interesting natural shape. Leave on one side to become firm.

Arrange and fix flowers and leaves together on the silver cardboard base securing with a little royal icing. Place a red candle in the centre and leave overnight to become firm. Then put in position on the cake.

Hot cross buns

scant $\frac{1}{2}$ pint milk
1 level teaspoon castor
   sugar
scant $\frac{1}{2}$ oz dried yeast
1 lb strong bread flour
1 level teaspoon salt
pinch mixed spice
pinch cinnamon
pinch nutmeg
2 oz castor sugar
4 oz currants
1 oz mixed chopped peel
1 egg, beaten
1 oz butter, melted
shortcrust pastry trimmings

scant 300 ml milk
1 level teaspoon castor
   sugar
scant 12.5 gm dried yeast
450 gm strong bread flour
1 level teaspoon salt
pinch mixed spice
pinch cinnamon
pinch nutmeg
50 gm castor sugar
100 gm currants
25 gm mixed chopped peel
1 egg, beaten
25 gm butter
shortcrust pastry trimmings

Heat the milk to hand hot and pour into a 1 pint (600 ml) measure. Add the level teaspoon castor sugar and yeast and whisk with a fork; leave for about 5 to 10 minutes until frothy.

Sift the flour with the salt and spices into a large bowl. Add the sugar and fruit. Stir the egg and butter into the yeast mixture, add the flour and mix well. This will make a soft dough.

Turn the dough onto a floured table and knead for about 10 minutes until smooth and no longer sticky, place in a lightly oiled polythene bag and leave to rise at room temperature for 1$\frac{1}{2}$ to 2 hours or until double in bulk.

Divide the dough into 12 pieces and shape into buns by using the palm of the hand, pressing down hard and then easing up. Place well spaced on a floured baking sheet. Put inside the oiled polythene bag and leave to rise at room temperature for about 1 hour until doubled in bulk.

Remove the bag. Roll out the pastry trimmings and cut into 24 strips about 4 inches (10 cm) long and $\frac{1}{4}$ inch (5 mm) wide, place two in a cross on each bun dampening the underside with water to make them stick. Bake in a hot oven 425°F,

For oven-fresh breakfast buns, cover the tray of shaped dough with a polythene bag and store in the fridge overnight. Remove and leave in a warm place until double the original size before baking.

220°C, Gas No. 7 for 15 to 20 minutes until golden brown.

Make a glaze by bringing 2 tablespoons water and 2 tablespoons milk to the boil, stirring in 1$\frac{1}{2}$ oz (40 gm) castor sugar and then boiling for 2 minutes. Remove the buns from the oven and glaze at once. Makes 12 buns.

Home-made white bread and rolls

just under ¾ pint hand-hot water
1 teaspoon sugar
½ oz dried yeast (3 level teaspoons)
1½ lb strong white flour
3 level teaspoons salt
½ oz lard

just under 450 ml hand-hot water
1 teaspoon sugar
12.5 gm dried yeast (3 level teaspoons)
675 gm strong white flour
3 level teaspoons salt
12.5 gm lard

Dissolve the sugar in the water, sprinkle on the yeast and leave for 10 to 15 minutes until frothy.

Put the flour and salt into a large bowl and rub in the lard; pour on the yeast liquid and mix well to a dough that will leave the sides of the bowl clean.

Turn onto a floured table and knead until smooth and no longer sticky. This will take about 10 minutes and is done by folding the dough towards you, then pushing down with the palm of the hand. Give the dough a quarter turn, repeat kneading developing a rocking rhythm and continue until the dough feels firm and elastic. Shape into a large ball, place in a large polythene bag greased with a little vegetable oil and leave in a warm place to rise until doubled in bulk. This will take about 1 hour in a warm place, 2 hours at room temperature or it may be left overnight in the refrigerator, in which case

the dough must be allowed to return to room temperature before shaping.

Turn the dough onto a lightly floured table and divide in half. Take one half of the dough and flatten with the knuckles to knock out the air, roll up like a Swiss roll and place in a greased loaf tin 7¾ inches (19.5 cm) by 4 inches (10 cm)* by 2¼ inches (6 cm). Put inside an oiled polythene bag and leave in a warm place until the dough rises to the top of the tin.

Divide the remaining dough into 9 pieces and shape into rolls. Place evenly spaced on a greased baking sheet, put in a greased polythene bag and leave until doubled in bulk.

Glaze the loaf and rolls with either salt and water, milk, water or a little beaten egg mixed with water or milk. Bake in a hot oven 450°F, 230°C, Gas No. 8 on the centre shelf. The rolls will need about 20 minutes cooking time and the loaf about 30 to 35 minutes. When done, the loaf will have shrunk slightly from the sides

of the tin and the crust will be a deep golden brown. To test, tap bread on the base: if ready it will sound hollow.

Cool on wire racks and then store in a polythene bag leaving the ends open. Makes 1 loaf and 9 bread rolls.

For the best results use the same sort of flour that the bakers use: strong plain flour, now available in most grocers and supermarkets. Dried yeast is easier to use than fresh and I find the results equally good. The yeast must froth up with the liquid and if it doesn't, this means the yeast is old and won't make the bread rise. Dried yeast may be stored in a tightly lidded container for up to 6 months.

Sugar and cinnamon bites

bread dough
castor sugar
cinnamon

Take a small quantity of bread dough, just enough to make 2 bread rolls, and shape into small balls.

Fry in hot deep fat or oil for about 2 minutes or until well risen and golden brown. Lift out with a slotted spoon and drain thoroughly on kitchen paper. Then toss in a little castor sugar mixed with cinnamon and serve straight away. Makes about 24 bites.

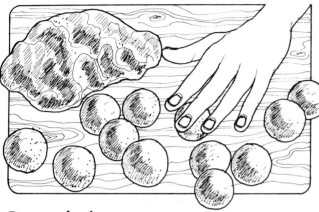

This makes a good way of using up dough trimmings.

Banana loaf

4 oz butter, softened
6 oz castor sugar
2 eggs, beaten
2 ripe bananas, mashed
8 oz plain flour
1 level teaspoon baking powder
1 level teaspoon bicarbonate of soda
2 tablespoons boiling milk

100 gm butter, softened
175 gm castor sugar
2 eggs, beaten
2 ripe bananas, mashed
225 gm plain flour
1 level teaspoon baking powder
1 level teaspoon bicarbonate of soda
2 tablespoons boiling milk

Heat the oven to 350°F, 180°C, Gas No. 4. and grease and line a 1lb (450 gm) loaf tin with greased greaseproof paper.

Cream the butter and sugar until light and fluffy and beat in the eggs and mashed bananas.

Sift the flour and baking powder together and stir the bicarbonate of soda into the milk. Then fold both into the creamed mixture. Turn into the tin and bake in the centre of the oven for 1 hour or until well risen and golden brown. Turn out and leave to cool on a wire rack with the paper removed. Serve just as it is or sliced and spread with butter.

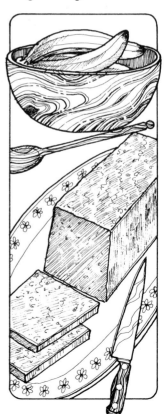

The last two bananas left in the fruit bowl often get over-ripe so that no one fancies them. At this stage they are perfect for this cake.

54

Express chocolate cake

6½ oz plain flour
2 tablespoons cocoa
1 level teaspoon
   bicarbonate of soda
1 level teaspoon baking
   powder
5 oz castor sugar
2 tablespoons golden syrup
2 eggs, lightly beaten
¼ pint corn oil
¼ pint milk
Fudge icing:
3 oz butter
2 oz cocoa, sieved
about 6 tablespoons milk
8 oz icing sugar, sieved

187 gm plain flour
2 tablespoons cocoa
1 level teaspoon bicarbonate
   of soda
1 level teaspoon baking
   powder
150 gm castor sugar
2 tablespoons golden syrup
2 eggs, lightly beaten
150 ml corn oil
150 ml milk
Fudge icing:
75 gm butter
50 gm cocoa, sieved
about 6 tablespoons milk
225 gm icing sugar, sieved

This cake keeps very well when filled with fudge icing. An alternative filling is a layer of apricot jam covered in fresh whipped cream. In this case store covered with clingwrap in the refrigerator and eat within 2 days.

Sieve the flour, cocoa, bicarbonate of soda and baking powder into a large bowl. Make a well in the centre and add the sugar and syrup. Gradually stir in the eggs, oil and milk and beat well to make a smooth batter.

Pour the batter into 2 greased 6 inch (20 cm) sandwich tins lined with greased greaseproof paper. Bake in the oven preheated to 325°F, 160°C, Gas No. 3 for 30 to 35 minutes or until the cakes spring back when lightly pressed with a fingertip. Turn cakes out onto a wire rack and leave to cool, removing the paper.

To make the icing: melt the butter in a small pan, stir in the cocoa and cook very gently for 1 minute. Remove the pan from the heat and stir in the milk and icing sugar. Mix well to a spreading consistency. Spread half the icing on one cake, then sandwich the cakes together and spread the remaining icing over the top of the cake. Leave to set. Decorate if liked.

Special apple dessert cake

5 oz butter
2 large eggs
8 oz castor sugar
1 teaspoon almond essence
8 oz self-raising flour
1½ level teaspoons baking powder
1½ lb cooking apples, before peeling
icing sugar

150 gm butter
2 large eggs
225 gm castor sugar
5 ml almond essence
225 gm self-raising flour
1.5 level teaspoons baking powder
675 gm cooking apples, before peeling
icing sugar

Heat the oven to 375°F, 190°C, Gas No. 5. Grease well a 10 inch (25 cm) loose-bottomed cake tin.

Melt the butter in a pan over a medium heat until just runny and pour into a large bowl. Add the eggs, sugar and almond essence and beat well until mixed. Fold in the flour and baking powder. Spread just under two thirds of the mixture in the cake tin. Then straight away peel, core and slice the apples and arrange roughly on top of the mixture. Spread the remaining mixture over the apples. It is difficult to get this last bit of mixture smooth, but don't worry as the blobs even out during cooking.

Bake for 1½ hours, until the apple is tender when prodded with a skewer. Loosen the sides of the cake with a knife and

This is highly delicious and very quick to make. You can serve it as a cake or a pudding. No need to prepare the apples ahead for this cake, just slice them fairly haphazardly straight onto the cake mixture, then quickly put the last bit of mixture over the top and bake.

carefully push the cake out.

Dust over very generously with icing sugar when slightly cooled and serve warm or cold with lots of lightly whipped or thick cream.

Keep covered in the fridge and eat within 4 days. Serves about 12.

Tasty tit-bits

Yum yums

8 oz soft margarine
6 oz castor sugar
1 egg, beaten
10 oz self-raising flour
2 oz cornflakes, lightly
   crushed

225 gm soft margarine
175 gm castor sugar
1 egg, beaten
275 gm self-raising flour
50 gm cornflakes, lightly
   crushed

Heat the oven to 375°F, 190°C, Gas No. 5 and grease 3 large baking sheets.

Put the margarine into a large bowl, add sugar and cream together with a wooden spoon until soft. Beat in the egg, then slowly work in the flour until the mixture has come together. If it is a warm day or the kitchen is hot the mixture may be rather soft to handle, so wrap it in cling film and chill for 10 minutes.

Wet the hands and lightly roll mixture into about 34 balls and roll each one in the crushed cornflakes. Position well spaced on the baking sheets and slightly flatten each with the hand. Bake for about 20 to 25 minutes until turning a very pale brown at the edges. Remove from the oven and leave on the trays for 1 minute before carefully lifting each biscuit onto a wire rack to cool. When quite cold store in an airtight tin. Makes about 34 Yum yums.

These are really good home-made biscuits and ideal for children to make from ingredients that you have in the store cupboard.

Scottish shortbread

6 oz plain flour
3 oz cornflour
6 oz butter
3 oz castor sugar

175 gm plain flour
75 gm cornflour
175 gm butter
75 gm castor sugar

Heat the oven to 325°F, 160°C, Gas No. 3.

Sift the flour and cornflour together. Cream the butter until soft. Add the sugar and beat until light and fluffy. Work in the flours then knead well together.

Press out the shortbread into a shallow greased baking tin 11 inches by 7 (28 cm by 17.5) flattening the dough with knuckles. Prick well with a fork and mark into 16 fingers with the back of a knife.

Chill in the refrigerator for 15 minutes, then bake in the oven for about 35 minutes or until a very pale golden brown. Leave to cool in the tin for 15 minutes then cut through where the shortbread is marked and then carefully lift onto a wire rack to finish cooling. Makes 16 pieces.

Butter is an absolute must for shortbread because the flavour really does come through. A proportion of cornflour, semolina and ground rice adds a crispy texture. Keep in an airtight tin.

▶ *(P. 58/59) Left to right:*
Yum yums, Scottish shortbread
and Crunchjacks

Crunchjacks

5 oz soft margarine
5 oz demerara sugar
5 oz quick porridge oats
1 oz desiccated coconut

150 gm soft margarine
150 gm demerara sugar
150 gm quick porridge oats
25 gm desiccated coconut

Heat the oven to 325°F, 160°C, Gas No. 3 and grease a shallow baking tin 11 inches by 7 (28 cm by 17.5).

Cream the margarine and sugar together until well blended and then stir in the oats and coconut and mix thoroughly.

Press into the tin and bake for 40 to 45 minutes until golden brown. Remove from the oven and leave for 10 minutes, then mark into 18 squares and leave to become quite cold in the tin.

Lift out of the tin and store in an airtight container. Makes 18 Crunch jacks.

When you are asked for goodies for a coffee morning or bazaar you can be sure that these will always go down well. They seem to be popular with all ages and never stay in the biscuit tin for long. To my mind they are rather nicer than flapjacks.

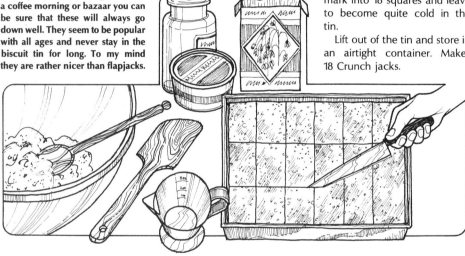

Lemon curd

2 oz butter
7 oz castor sugar
2 lemons
4 egg yolks, beaten

50 gm butter
200 gm castor sugar
2 lemons
4 egg yolks, beaten

This is one preserve that is well worth making at home. Though it's not cheap it's very good and a clever way of using up yolks after a meringue-making session.

Place the butter and sugar in the top of a double saucepan with simmering water in the lower part. If you do not have a double saucepan, use a basin over a pan of water. Stir well until the butter has melted.

Stir the finely grated rind and the juice from the lemons into the pan together with the egg yolks. Continue to stir over the simmering water until the curd thickens: this will take about 20 to 25 minutes. Remove from the heat and pour the lemon curd into clean warm jars, cover and seal while hot and label when cold.

Keep in a cool larder for 4 weeks or in the refrigerator for 3 months. Makes a 1 lb (450 gm) or two ½ lb (225 gm) jars.

Mincemeat

It is worth getting stoned raisins for mincemeat as they have a much better flavour than the stoneless ones. I remember as a child our small grocer had a machine that took the stones out rather like a huge mechanical parsley mincer— you turned a handle and the pips dropped out underneath and rather squashy seeded raisins came out at the other end. At Christmas the machine had to work overtime.

1½ lb stoned raisins
¼ lb candied peel
1 lb cooking apples
¾ lb currants
½ lb sultanas
6 oz shredded suet
½ level teaspoon mixed spice
2 lemons
1 lb soft brown sugar
6 tablespoons rum, brandy
  or sherry

675 gm stoned raisins
100 gm candied peel
450 gm cooking apples
350 gm currants
225 gm sultanas
175 gm shredded suet
½ level teaspoon mixed spice
2 lemons
450 gm soft brown sugar
6 tablespoons rum, brandy
  or sherry

Finely chop or mince the raisins and peel. Peel, core and mince or chop the apples. Place in a large bowl with the other fruit, suet and spice. Grate the rind and squeeze the juice from the lemons, add with the sugar and rum, brandy or sherry to the fruit and mix very well.

Cover the bowl with a cloth and leave to stand overnight. Next day turn into clean jars, cover and label. Makes about 5½ lb (2.5 kg).

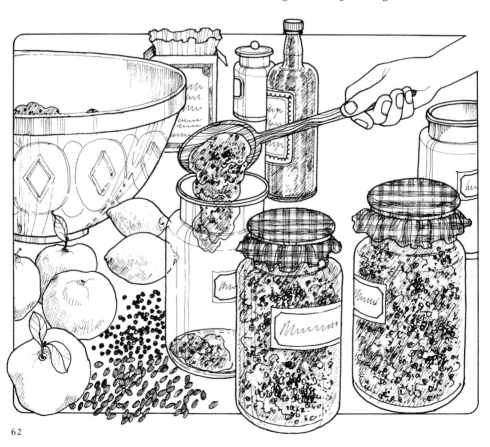

Index

Almond paste, 50
Apple
    dessert cake, special, 56
    jelly, with grapes, 36
Apricots with roast chicken and nut
    stuffing, 14

Bacon-stuffed hearts, 21
Banana loaf, 54
Beef cassoulet, spicy, 18
Blackberry mousse, 39
Bread and rolls, home-made white,
    53
Brussels sprouts in Frugal soup, 8

Cake(s)
    Christmas, 48
    express chocolate, 55
    marmalade fruit, 47
    special apple dessert, 56
Carrot soup, 6
Cassoulet, spicy beef, 18
Cheese
    aigrettes, 10
    soufflé, 9
Cheesecake, quick lemon, 40
Chestnut stuffing with watercress, 23
Chicken
    galantine, 13
    curry, with cream and grapes, 15
    paprika, 12
    roast, with apricots and nut
        stuffing, 14
Chipped potatoes, 24
Chocolate
    cake, express, 55
    and orange mousse, 35
    soufflé, 31
Christmas cake
    icing the, 50
    with pineapple, 49
Christmas pudding, 30
Christmas roses, 51
Cream
    with mild chicken curry, 15
    in soup, 6

Crunchjacks, 60
Cucumber and dill salad, 28
Curried egg mayonnaise, 28
Curry, mild chicken, with cream and
    grapes, 15

Dill and cucumber salad, 28

Egg mayonnaise, curried, 28
Express chocolate cake, 55

Flan, Thomas's, 42
French country casserole or pie, 16
French vegetable quiche, 25
Frugal soup, 8
Fruitcake, marmalade, 47
Fruit salad, rosy red, 36

Galantine, chicken, 13
Gooseberry fool, 40
Grapes
    with apple jelly, 36
    with mild chicken curry, 15

Ham rolls, 28
Hearts, bacon-stuffed, 21
Hot cross buns, 52
Hot pot, lamb, 17

Ice cream
    lemon, 43
    praline, 43
Icing
    chocolate fudge, 55
    the Christmas cake, 50
    Christmas roses, 51
    royal, 50

Jelly, apple, with grapes, 36

Lamb hot pot, 17
Lamb's hearts, bacon-stuffed, 21
Lamb's liver in onion sauce, 20
Leek soup, fresh, 6
Lemon
    cheesecake, quick, 40
    curd, 60
    ice cream, 43
    mousse, quick, 38
    soufflé pudding, 32
Liver in onion sauce, 20

Marmalade fruitcake, 47
Mayonnaise, curried egg, 28
Melon
    mint sorbet, 46

and prawns in sour cream, 11
Mincemeat, 62
Mince pie, 32
Mint and melon sorbet, 46
Mousse
    blackberry, 39
    chocolate and orange, 35
    quick lemon, 38

Niçoise salad, 27
Nut stuffing with roast chicken, 14

Onion
    sauce, 20
    and tomato salad, 28
Oxtail, 19

Paprika chicken, 12
Pavlova, 34
Pig's liver in onion sauce, 20
Pineapple with Christmas cake, 49
Potatoes, chipped, 24
Praline ice cream, 43
Prawns and melon in sour cream, 11

Quiche, French vegetable, 25

Raspberry pavlova, 34
Ratatouille, 27
Rosy red fruit salad, 36
Royal icing, 50-1

Salad(s)
    cucumber and dill, 28
    Niçoise, 27
    Swedish platter, 28
    tomato and onion, 28
Sausage, lemon and thyme stuffing,
    23
Scottish shortbread, 57
Sorbet, melon mint, 46
Soufflé(s)
    cheese, 9
    chocolate, 31
    lemon pudding, 32
    omelette, 29
Soup
    fresh leek, 6
    frugal, 8
    good carrot, 6
Sour cream, melon and prawns in, 11
Spicy beef cassoulet, 18
Stuffing
    chestnut, 23
    nut, 14
    sausage, lemon and thyme, 23

Sugar and cinnamon bites, 54
Swedish salad platter, 28

Thomas's flan, 42
Tomato and onion salad, 28
Turkey roast, classic, 22

Vegetable quiche, French, 25

Watercress, with chestnut stuffing,
   23

Yum yums, 57

Credits

Artist
Bill McLaughlin
Photographer
John Lee
Home economist
Rosemary Wadey
Cover design
Camron
Cover photograph
John Lee